Times Change

At Play

Long Ago and Today

Lynnette R. Brent

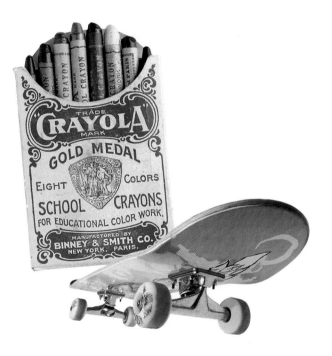

Heinemann Library
Chicago, Illinois

Design by Herman Adler Design
Editorial Development by
Morrison BookWorks, LLC
Photo research by Carol Parden,
Image Resources
Printed and bound in the United States by
Lake Book Manufacturing, Inc.

07 06 05 04
10 9 8 7 6 5 4 3 2

Library of Congress Cataloging-in-Publication Data
Brent, Lynnette R., 1965-
At play: long ago and today / Lynnette R. Brent.
    p. cm. -- (Times change)
Summary: An introduction to how children's
and adult's leisure activities have changed in
the past one hundred years, discussing how
people play and relax at different times of the
year, on special occasions, and on vacation.
Includes bibliographical references and index.
    ISBN 1-4034-4532-X (Library Binding-hard-cover) -- ISBN 1-4034-4538-9 (Paperback)

1. Play--History--Juvenile literature.
2. Recreation--History--Juvenile literature.
[1. Play--History. 2. Recreation--History.]
I. Title. II. Series
  GV45.B74 2003
  790.1--dc21
                              2003011030

Acknowledgments
The author and publishers are grateful to
the following for permission to reproduce
copyright material: pp. 1(t-l), 16(b), 30(b-l)
Benny & Smith Inc.; pp. 1(b-l), 6(b), 30(b-m)
Comstock Klips; p. 4 Bettmann/Corbis; p. 5
Hulton-Deutsch Collection/Corbis; pp. 6, 8, 14,
16(t), 22 Brown Brothers; p. 7 Diaphor Agency/
Index Stock Imagery; p. 9 David R. Frazier/
Frazier Photolibrary; pp. 10(t), 12 Culver
Pictures; p. 10 (b) Point Mallard Park;
p. 11 Daniel Mier/ Corbis; pp. 13, 29 Tony
Freeman/PhotoEdit; p. 15 Tim Thompson/
Corbis; pp.17, 21 Digital Stock; pp.18(t), 24(t),
26 Corbis; p. 18 (b) Photodisc; p. 19 Michael
Newman/PhotoEdit; p. 22 (b) Sears Archives;
p. 23 PictureQuest; p. 25 Roy Morsch/Corbis; p.
27 Ray Juno/Corbis; p. 28 Circus World
Museum, Baraboo, WI

Cover photographs reproduced with permission
of (t) Brown Brothers, (b) Will Hart/PhotoEdit

Every effort has been made to contact
copyright holders of any material reproduced
in this book. Any omissions will be rectified
in subsequent printings if notice is given to
the publisher.

Some words are shown in bold, **like this.**
You can find out what they mean by looking
in the glossary.

Contents

Long Ago

Imagine that it is long ago. You have just finished listening to your favorite radio show. Now you are making your own scooter with the wheels from your old roller skates and a piece of wood your dad gave you.

Your friends are calling you from outside! It is time for you to try the scooter you have made. You run outside and meet your friends. They love the new scooter!

This is what you may have been doing if you lived 100 years ago. What else would you have been doing with your friends and family long ago? Let's see what Americans did to play long ago.

Long ago, children made their own scooters or rented them with their friends.

57

PRAM
TYRES
WIRED
ON.

ALL
REPAIRS

CYCLES
&
SCOOTERS
FOR
HIRE.

Fun Ways to Get Around

Long ago, most children walked to where they wanted to go. But some children had fun ways to get around. Many had roller skates. Fewer children had bicycles because bicycles cost a lot of money. Some children made their own scooters with wood and old roller skate parts.

Long ago, roller skates were clamped right onto children's shoes.

Times Change

What Changed in 1958?

In 1958, the first skateboard was created in California. It was made for people to go "sidewalk **surfing**" when they could not surf in the ocean.

Pads help keep children safe as they get around.

Today, children have many fun ways to get around. Children can still walk, ride bicycles, or use roller skates. Children also still use scooters, but now scooters are made of metal and are bought from the store. Many children also like to skateboard and rollerblade.

Playing Sports

Long ago, children played many sports. Boys mostly played stickball, basketball, football, and field hockey. Girls mostly played tennis, golf, and **croquet.**

Children usually played together in their own neighborhoods. They did not have special times of the year for each sport.

Stickball was played with a broomstick and a small ball.

Today, children still play sports that were played long ago. But now, both boys and girls play many of the same sports, like basketball or tennis.

Many children play sports in community programs or for their school teams. Children play different sports at different times of the year.

Girls and boys play baseball during spring and summer.

Hot Weather Fun

Rivers and lakes were places to keep cool.

Long ago, a good way to stay cool when it was hot outdoors was to go swimming. Children went to a swimming hole or beach with lots of other children. Everyone had to be very careful, because there were no **lifeguards** to watch out for them.

Times Change

What Changed in 1970?

In August of 1970, the first wave pool opened at Point Mallard Park in Decatur, Alabama. Motors in the pool created waves three feet high.

Wave pools, water slides, and waterfalls help people cool off at Point Mallard Park.

Wisconsin is home to the largest water park in the United States.

Today, children still like to go swimming when it is hot outdoors. Besides beaches, children can swim at pools and water parks. There are lifeguards at beaches, pools, and water parks today. Lifeguards have special training to keep people safe.

Enjoying the Park

Long ago, families enjoyed spending time together at the park. They took strolls, talked with friends, or just relaxed. They sometimes packed a picnic lunch and spent an entire afternoon at the park eating and having fun.

Central Park in New York was the first public park in the United States.

Today, parks like this one are found all around the United States.

Today, families still enjoy spending time together at the park. Now, parks have more to offer, like slides, swings, jungle gyms, softball diamonds, or basketball courts. Many families still pack picnic lunches before they go to the park. Sometimes, they have a **barbeque** and cook food on a grill.

Cold Weather Fun

Children had to dress warmly to enjoy cold-weather activities outdoors.

Long ago, winter was the only time of year that children could do cold-weather activities. For example, they went ice-skating on frozen ponds or lakes. When it snowed, they rode down hills on wooden sleds.

Today, children can enjoy some cold-weather activities all year long. For example, they can ice-skate on indoor ice rinks in any season. Sledding, in most places, can still be done only in the winter. Today's sleds are not always made of wood. Often, they are made of plastic.

Refrigerated pipes keep ice frozen indoors all year long.

Arts and Crafts

Long ago, boys made boats like these from scraps of wood and cloth.

Long ago, children used household items to make arts and crafts. Girls made their own dolls from old cloth, wood, or even cornhusks. Boys made model boats and trains out of wood.

Times Change

What Changed in 1903?

In 1903, the first crayons were invented. They were invented so people could have art supplies that were not expensive.

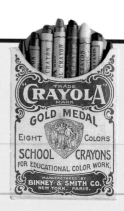

Today, there are many types of art supplies for children to use.

Today, children can buy kits to make dolls, models, or other kinds of toys at arts and crafts stores. Stores also sell art supplies like markers, paint, and **glitter** pens. Children today can use these supplies to decorate arts and crafts projects.

Games

Ringer and Rolley-hole were popular marble games.

Long ago, people played different kinds of games. Board games, like checkers, were a popular family activity. Marbles was a game that children liked to play with their friends. To play this game, children bounced their marbles against other marbles in a circle. They won any marbles they could knock out of the circle.

Times Change

What Changed in 1972?

In 1972, the first electronic TV video game was sold. It was called Odyssey and had 12 games people could play such as Math-a-Magic, Buzzword, and many sports games.

Today, people still play many of the same games that were played long ago, such as checkers and marbles. But now, video games are also popular. Many children like to play video games on their televisions or on their computers. Some even have handheld video games that are so small they can be played anywhere!

Children can play sports, adventure, or puzzle video games.

Reading

Reading was a favorite family pasttime.

Long ago, reading was something that families did together. Usually, one person in the family read aloud while the other family members listened.

Most families owned just a few books because books were very expensive. Many towns did not have libraries. This meant families would read the same stories again and again.

Today, families still read together. Many children read with their parents before they go to bed at night. Many people enjoy listening to books that are recorded on tape or compact disc (CD).

Today, because books cost less, families own more books than they did long ago. Also, people can get books from many places. Bookstores and libraries are popular places for people to find new books.

Sometimes, family members take turns reading aloud.

Watching Movies

Long ago, children did not watch movies at home. They would go to places called nickelodeons. Nickelodeons were the first real movie theaters in the United States. The first nickelodeon opened in 1905, and one show cost a nickel. The movies were short and had no sound.

Films were mostly about fashion or current events.

Times Change

What Changed in 1972?

In 1972, the first videocassette recorder for the home was invented. The videocassette recorder, or VCR, let people watch movies at home at a time they decided.

The AVCO Cartrivision was the first VCR.

Today, there are many choices for watching movies. Families can watch movies at movie theaters or on television. Children can watch movies on videotapes, digital video discs (DVDs), or on their computers. Families can buy movies at many different stores. They can also rent them from stores or even from libraries.

At home, families can choose to watch movies or other programs.

Listening to Music

Long ago, people usually made their own music. Children sang or played instruments for the rest of the family. Sometimes families went to concerts or dances where they listened to other people sing or play instruments for them. A few families had gramophones that could play recorded music.

A gramophone is an old-time record player.

Times Change

What Changed in 1920?

In 1920, radio stations started to **broadcast** radio programs. A radio station in Montreal was the first to broadcast a scheduled musical program. It was a concert by a singer named Dorothy Lutton.

People can choose from many different types of music.

Today, people have many choices for listening to music. Many children still play instruments. They might take lessons or play in a school band. Some children like listening to music on the radio or CD players. Many children like watching television to see their favorite performers sing or play instruments. Families still go to concerts today.

Family Vacations

Some families spent their vacations swimming or boating.

Long ago, few families took vacations. If they did, they went camping in a nearby forest or visited beaches that were close to home. There were few roads, so people could not easily travel to the places they wanted to go.

Times Change

What Changed in 1956?

In 1956, Congress passed the Interstate Highway Act. Because of this law, many new highways were built. On these new highways, people could drive to many more places than they could before.

Today, more families go on vacation because traveling is easier. There are many more roads across the country. People can drive their cars to places that are far from home. Some families travel by train or by airplane. By taking cars, trains, and airplanes, families have many choices of vacation locations.

Many families take vacations all over the world.

Special Events

Long ago, there were many special events children looked forward to. One was the circus coming to town! Children would line the streets with their parents to see the animals and clowns walk through the town. Some towns even had carnivals. Carnivals were a place for people to ride the **Ferris wheel,** eat food, and play games.

Circus parades let people know the circus was in town.

Children of all ages enjoy roller coasters.

Today, children enjoy some of the same events as long ago. Some children go to the circus when it comes to town. The carnival is still a place for families to have fun. Now, many children go to theme parks where fast roller coasters and merry-go-rounds are very popular.

You have seen how Americans played long ago. People played games with friends, went swimming in warm weather, and went ice skating in cold weather. People spent long afternoons in the park and took vacations to places near their homes.

Today, people do these things and more. Today, people can play video games on a computer or play in a water park. They can enjoy swings and slides in parks and travel to places that are far from home.

Times Change

1903	1920	1956	1958	1970	1972
Crayola Crayons are invented.	A radio station **broadcasts** the first scheduled music program.	Congress passes the Interstate Highway Act.	The first skateboard is invented.	The first wave pool is opened.	The first electronic video game is sold. The first videocassette recorder (VCR) for the home is invented.

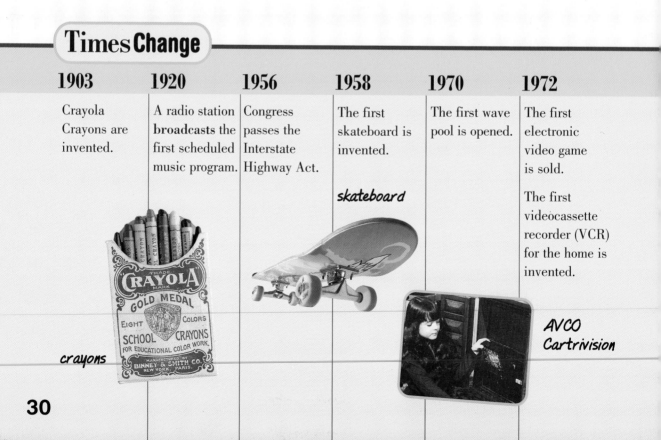

skateboard

crayons

AVCO Cartrivision

Glossary

barbeque meal cooked outdoors over an open fire

broadcast to send out music, news, or other programs by radio

croquet outdoor game played with sticks used to hit wooden balls through wire hoops

Ferris wheel tall carnival ride shaped like a wheel

glitter small pieces of shiny material used to decorate crafts

lifeguard person who works at a beach or pool that helps and protects swimmers

surfing riding on a wave with a long board

More Books to Read

King, David. *World War II Days: Discover the Past With Exciting Projects, Games, Activities, and Recipes (American Kids in History Series).* John Wiley. New York, 2000.

Murphy, Frank. *The Legend of the Teddy Bear.* Sleeping Bear Press. Chelsea, MI 2000.

Steele, Philip. *Toys and Games (Everyday History).* Franklin Watts, Inc. New York, 2000.

Index